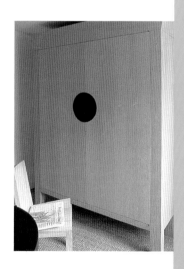

MAKING
THE MOST OF
WORK
SPACES

MAKING
THE MOST OF
WORK
SPACES

LORRIE MACK

CONRAN OCTOPUS

FOR BRIAN

Project Editor   Jane Chapman
Art Editor   Alistair Plumb
Picture Research   Claire Taylor
Production   Julia Golding
Illustrator   Sarah John

First published in 1995 by
Conran Octopus Limited
37 Shelton Street
London WC2H 9HN

Reprinted 1996

British Library Cataloguing-in-Publication Data
A catalogue record for this book is available from the British Library

ISBN 1 85029 721 5

Printed in Hong Kong

CONTENTS

The sleek, professional look of this stylish home-office-cum-library has been achieved by choosing the same matt-black finish for all the main elements: the bookshelves backed with matching panels, the cantilevered display surface, the floor-standing cupboards and the sculptural desk that occupies the room's central position.

The storage system covers the walls completely, making maximum use of the available space, and its individual components have been designed to do the same; the distance between each bookshelf, for example, is slightly different, to cater for volumes of varying size, and all the cupboards have sliding doors, which do not require any space for clearance, or protrude dangerously into the narrow traffic path.

INTRODUCTION

The dramatic rise in the number of people who now work at home in some capacity is one of the most significant social changes of the twentieth century. This shift is largely the result of advances in computer and communications technology, combined with an increasingly unstable job market and the high proportion of women who now return to the job market after the birth of their children. Of the millions of people who work at home, some do so because they have no other option, but many more choose this way of life because, for them, it is not only the most convenient, it is also the most profitable, and by far the most fulfilling.

To cope with this change, a whole new sector has evolved within the office-equipment industry to meet the needs of a very real, and previously very neglected, gap in the market for basic, up-to-date equipment and machines that are sufficiently compact, simple and cheap to meet the needs of small businesses and the self-employed.

But it's not only clerical occupations that are carried out from home; small-scale creative and craft-based trades are often required to share domestic accommodation. In addition, many hobbies require their own purpose-designed space, and even mundane chores like writing letters, paying bills and keeping household accounts become more appealing when a suitable and well-organized area has been set aside for them.

While institutional work spaces are designed and furnished by professionals with specialist knowledge and large budgets, however, those at home often tend to be thrown together haphazardly, and fitted out with bits and pieces bought cheaply, borrowed from other rooms or donated by friends. Too often, this approach produces inferior and inappropriate facilities that, at best, make working from home a frustrating and depressing experience; at worst, they can also reduce your productivity dramatically, and inflict serious and permanent damage on your health.

Fortunately, however, creating a stylish, efficient and comfortable work space need not be expensive or difficult. With the right knowledge, a little common sense and a lot of imagination, you can transform even the least prepossessing corner into a totally functional environment that is a pleasure to be in at the same time.

PLANNING

When you are unhappy with any part of your home, the problem is often poor planning – or even lack of planning altogether. While most people devote some degree of care to the design of a living room or bedroom, however, work spaces are often thrown together with little regard for the way they will look or function. In fact, when you think through every detail in advance, you're well on the way to creating a home office or studio that fulfils your needs and lives up to all your expectations.

A BLUEPRINT FOR SUCCESS

The concept of work done at home can encompass a vast and varied range of activities, from running a small computer-based business to dressmaking, painting, making jewellery or simply ploughing through day-to-day domestic paperwork. Whatever form your work takes, you'll find it much easier to deal with if the space you set aside for it is comfortable, efficient, attractive and safe, and the only way to make sure all these criteria are met is by investing a little careful and informed planning.

Choosing a location

You first need to decide where your work space is going to be; is it possible to set aside a separate room, or will you have to adapt part of an existing one? If all you need is a place to write letters, pay bills or mount stamps, then a well-organized desk in a quiet corner would be more than adequate. The situation becomes more complex, however, when you have to accommodate a full-time occupation or a particularly space- or time-consuming hobby.

In some homes, there may be an extra room that can be commandeered, or unused space that would lend itself to conversion, such as a basement, attic, garage, conservatory or even a roomy walk-in cupboard or closet. If any of your rooms are high enough, you could consider installing a cantilevered gallery or mezzanine level to house your office or studio. Explore the potential of under-used areas such as a wide landing or a generously proportioned entrance hall.

One of the most common arrangements is for a home work space to share its floor area with one or more other activities. If this is the obvious solution for you, take time to work out which ones can be combined most successfully. The ideal arrangement is to set up your work area in a room that is not in daily use: a guest bedroom perhaps, or a dining room that is occupied only on special occasions (the rest of the time, the table could do double duty as a desk). If there are no such part-time rooms available, you will have to adapt one of the main ones.

When it comes to deciding which room to choose, one of the most obvious considerations is space; the biggest room should, in theory, be able to cater for the most activity, but space is not the only thing to bear in mind, and sometimes it isn't even the most important. It may seem sensible, for example, to slot your office into the master bedroom, which in any case is occupied only at night. For many people, this might work perfectly, but others may find it difficult to unwind in a room so strongly associated with the pressures and panics of a working day. Similarly, if your occupation requires quiet and privacy, locating a work area in the family kitchen, however spacious, is likely to prove totally impractical.

Once you have decided which room to work in, see if there is a particular architectural feature that lends itself to the purpose. The short arm of an L-shape would be a natural choice, for example, as would one end of a long, narrow room; in both of these cases, it might be possible to divide this part of the room from the rest with sliding doors or a floor-to-ceiling curtain. Alternatively, define it more subtly with a judiciously placed item of furniture, such as a tall screen, a free-standing bookshelf or even just a

WORKING RECESSES

Abundant natural light, generous proportions and the existence of two deep alcoves make this lofty living room (left) an ideal location for a compact, convenient home office. Set into the sunniest recess, the desk is a built-in shelf with a drawer pedestal attached; this neat unit affords maximum surface and storage space, yet leaves the floor completely clear.

Despite the amount of activity carried on here, this room has a clean, graphic look achieved by concealing all extraneous clutter behind closed doors; a run of roomy cupboards extends right across both alcoves and above the fireplace. Storage facilities are allocated on the basis of accessibility: reference books that are in constant use live just above floor level, while an inspiring frieze and architectural models dominate the room from on high.

The owner of this pristine, all-white bedroom (previous page, left) has used the same tactic of extending the work surface out beyond the alcove to provide maximum space.

On a much smaller scale, a deep window recess provides an ideal location for this compact, sunny home office (previous page, right).

A SUITABLE SITE

People who carry on a full-time occupation from home have much more complex work-space requirements than those whose main need is for a place to deal with domestic paperwork. The work area in this basement (left), for example, is ideal for small-scale tasks, but completely unsuitable for professional use: there is no direct lighting on the desk, the storage facilities are almost non-existent and the folding director's chair was never intended to provide adequate support over long periods.

The office situated in this light and airy room (right, above), however, has been planned to fulfil a much more serious function: the L-shaped desk has a large surface area and two drawer pedestals that, together with the nearby cupboard, accommodate a vast amount of paraphernalia. Two desk lamps provide more than adequate illumination and the traditional wooden chair, while not ergonomically ideal, was at least designed for its purpose.

If your administrative tasks are few, try tucking your office into the otherwise wasted space under the stairs (right). Here, a desk and shelf fixed to tongue-and-groove cladding make excellent use of a tiny, awkward corner. Create an illusion of space and a custom-made look by choosing an all-over timber or paint finish that matches the handrail, newel post and balusters. To keep your work surface clear, opt for a wall-fixed desk lamp, or one that clips onto the edge of the shelf.

high-backed sofa. This idea would work equally well to set off another obvious site for a work area: a deep alcove into which a desk with shelves above it can be fitted neatly.

Dividing multi-purpose spaces in this way not only creates a more private and distraction-free environment, it also deals with one of the major drawbacks of such compromises – the question of clutter. An unavoidable jumble of work-in-progress is unlikely to enhance any room's style, but you will quickly tire of clearing away your paperwork or materials at the end of every day, only to face unpacking it all again the next morning. A more informal camouflage tactic is to hang some kind of small blind or curtain that you can draw over the chaos when you finish, or just drape it with a huge square of fabric that blends unobtrusively into your scheme.

WORK-SPACE INVENTORY

- Work surface: for most tasks, the optimum size is about 150 x 85cm (59 x 33in).

- Seating: will you have to cater for visitors? If there isn't room for more than one chair, invest in a few folding designs – some can even be hung on the wall.

- Storage: compile a detailed list of requirements; specifying simply 'books' won't tell you how much room they'll occupy. Establish whether you have to order (and therefore store) a minimum quantity of any specific materials or stationery, and work out in advance how much filing you'll need access to, and how much can be stored elsewhere.

- Equipment: will you have a telephone, fax, answering machine, computer, photocopier, light box, sewing machine, electric kettle, etc? If you use electrical equipment, especially if it produces a lot of heat (a welding iron for making jewellery, for example), you should add a fire extinguisher to your list. Also bear in mind that computers dry the atmosphere considerably, so a small humidifier might be a good idea.

STORAGE SOLUTIONS

Make sure that all equipment and supplies in regular use are kept within easy reach. The two capacious storage pedestals that support the huge desk in this living room (left) swallow up stationery, files and small items of office equipment so that its surface can be used largely for display.

When space is at a premium, invest in a large trolley that can accommodate all your professional necessities and be tucked neatly away when it's not required. The curved work surface ingeniously fixed in this tight corner (right) would be impractical without the storage facilities provided by this spacious wooden model.

Assessing your needs

Once you have established where your work space is to go, compile a list of everything that will be required to fit into it. Your basic requirements will be a surface, a chair, some kind of storage furniture and whatever equipment and materials are involved in your activity. (Remember that you may be able to make the best use of the available space with a fitted, built-in work surface instead of a free-standing desk or table.) One important function of this list is to reveal how much and what kind of storage capacity you will require – books and box files will need sturdy shelves, for example, computer disks should be kept in covered boxes and voluminous correspondence is most accessible in filing drawers.

Work out which items will be in constant use, and need to be within easy reach, and which can be located further away. If you're constantly on the telephone, for example, you'll waste a great deal of time if you have to get up and walk across the room to use it, whereas if you only make two or three calls a day, moving the phone off your desk could free valuable space. Similarly, a fax machine that constantly hums with vital messages needs to be close at hand, but if faxes come and go rarely, and they tend not to be urgent, the machine could even be installed in a different room. If, on the other hand, your office or studio is a long way from the kitchen, squeezing some basic tea- or coffee-making facilities into your plans will save you endless time-wasting, concentration-shattering journeys.

DIVIDE AND CONQUER

Originally invented to shut out icy draughts and afford a degree of privacy, hinged screens are ideal for defining a work space within a larger area, and for disguising unsightly disarray.

You can buy – or make – these screens in a wide range of different styles and sizes to suit both your requirements and the personality and proportions of your room.

The simplest screens are constructed from several flat panels made from either finished wood or fabric-covered board, often with a thin layer of padding to give a soft, textured look. The more elaborate versions consist of several frames onto which widths of fabric have been gathered.

In most domestic settings, three panels are usually quite adequate, but if you want a higher screen – to conceal a row of untidy shelves perhaps – you will also have to increase its width (and therefore the number of panels) in order to ensure stability.

In this dual-purpose bedroom (above), a basic screen covered in plain blue fabric helps to partition off the efficient L-shaped work surface at the close of the working day, making it easier for the space to assume its more tranquil night-time persona. The screen fits in well with the rest of the room's decor, but if your decorating scheme has a period or a country flavour, choose a gathered screen in a floral print, a figured brocade or a set of matching lace panels.

TRANSFORMATION SCHEME

Concealed behind these six elegant panels are all the equipment and accessories needed to turn a comfortable dining room into a spacious, well-appointed home office. Constructed of warm, natural wood to blend effortlessly with the rest of the scheme, this versatile screen folds up flat when it's not in use, and stands unobtrusively against the wall until meal time comes around once more.

Note, too, the matching storage unit with cantilevered shelves that appear to have no means of support.

For dual-purpose rooms like this one, plain, neutral colours and practical materials such as metal, wood, cotton and sisal are always a wise choice.

■ 17

WORKING WALL

This large studio flat provides a base for a small media-related business. In order to house all the basic services (electricity, telecommunications, plumbing and waste) neatly and efficiently, and to separate leisure spaces from those designed for work, the architect has set the kitchen, the audio/visual centre and the office area side by side along one wall.

Tied together visually by a strong, simple black-and-white colour scheme, all the sections have been carefully planned to accommodate the necessary equipment and materials, and organized for maximum ease of use. The choice of practical, hard-wearing surfaces such as vinyl flooring, ceramic wall tiles and laminate work surfaces ensures that maintenance is kept to a minimum.

If you work in a separate room and either require complete quiet and privacy (for counselling perhaps), or produce an irritating volume of noise (drilling or hammering for example), it is worth considering some form of sound insulation. This can involve sophisticated installations such as double doors or a special lining on the walls, but a long interlined curtain across the door, or a layer of thick cork tiles, tongue-and-groove cladding or felt-covered fibre-board on the walls would also be very effective. Remember, too, that solidly packed bookshelves running from wall to wall and ceiling to floor can provide another valuable form of insulation.

Organizing your space

In order to work out what should go where, you will need to establish the dimensions of all the major furnishing elements: desk, chair, filing cabinet, bookshelves, etc. The time-honoured trick of cutting out shapes to scale and arranging them on an accurate floor plan can often help you avoid mistakes. Don't forget, however, to take into account the clearance each item requires for maximum comfort and safety in use. An office chair, for instance, should have about 1m (3ft 3in) of floor space between its desk and another piece of furniture (or a wall) so you can get in and out easily. You should also allow 1m (3ft 3in) in

DESIGNER DETAILS

Few people can afford a luxurious, custom-built office like this one, but some of its most successful elements could easily be adapted to suit more modest facilities. The fitted shelves, for example, are constructed with matching uprights that form neat squares and rectangles; these not only provide compact and organized storage compartments, they also add subtle visual detail.

At the window, a simple blind eliminates glare when the sun's rays are too strong. Most of the time, though, it rolls away out of sight, taking up little space, obscuring no light and leaving the spectacular view completely intact.

front of a filing cabinet for convenient access to the drawers, while 90cm (36in) is usually enough in front of a row of shelves. These figures may be tempting to ignore, but if you end up banging your head every time you bend to get a book from a low shelf, you may wish you had shown them more respect.

Another useful measurement is the distance most people can reach across a work surface from a sitting position: the most comfortable zone is within about 75cm (30in), so try to locate within this area the items that will be in constant use, such as the keyboard, telephone and writing equipment. The space immediately beyond this – between 75 and 95cm (30 and 38in) – can be reached only by stretching, and is therefore better suited for things that are used less often, such as filing trays. Those fortunate enough to have a desk deeper than 95cm (38in) will probably have to stand to get at anything arranged along its edge.

Where a surface is particularly small and cluttered, you may be able to improve the situation by investing in a wall-mounted telephone. If your desk butts up against a wall, you could even sit a computer screen on a wall-fixed shelf that can be positioned at your chosen height; these ingenious devices pivot into place in front of you, then fold out of the way when they're not in use.

Another practical idea is to sweep some of your paraphernalia off the surface altogether and onto a wheeled trolley. Choose either a purpose-made design with small drawers and trays, or a standard catering model with two roomy shelves. At the end of the day, this efficient storage item can be rolled away out of sight, perhaps even under the desk.

NATURAL LINKS

A work space that forms part of a
larger room should harmonize with
its surroundings. Here, an efficiently
organized and well-equipped design
studio has been installed at one end
of a light and spacious living room.
Redeployed from its previous position
in an old school or public library, the
gigantic table acts as a vast work
surface, has generous storage facilities
on top and in its many drawers, and sets
the office space apart from the rest of
the living area.

Used throughout, large expanses of
natural, earthy colour and texture –
creamy walls, golden polished wood
and chestnut-hued quarry tiles – create
a warm, inviting atmosphere, provide an
ideal background for both commercial
and decorative accessories, and link the
two activity areas visually.

MULTIPLICATION TABLE

When several different activities jostle for space in the same household, solve the problem by investing in one large, sturdy table; then provide enough concealed storage facilities nearby to cater for each different occupation, hobby or domestic function.

This expansive run of fitted storage units is divided into several separate sections, each one designed for a different purpose. After meals, when all the china, glass and cutlery have been returned to their designated shelves, the large dining table assumes its other identity as a dressmaker's cutting table. The sewing machine sits on a hinged work surface that folds neatly away behind huge sliding doors when it is not in use.

SLIDING SOLUTIONS

Install a large pair of custom-made sliding doors to create a totally separate work space within a larger area. Although these will be more expensive than a row of shelves and a desk, they will still cost far less than building an extension, or adding an internal wall.

This ingenious U-shaped home office (left) steals very little floor space from the family living room, yet allows everything in it – the wall-mounted computer, the work surface with its integral keyboard drawer, the angled drawing board and the roomy cube storage system – to be positioned within easy reach.

Planning for comfort and safety

It is only in the last few years, as the computer has begun to dominate the workplace, that the need for sound ergonomic planning has become widely recognized. Many of the basic principles, however, are really just a matter of sound common sense, and could be applied to a wide range of different occupations.

Positioning your screen at the right height, for example, prevents the constant back and shoulder tension that is almost inevitable when you spend hours with your neck slightly inclined. In the same way, a painter's easel is adjustable in height, and moving it just enough so you can work with your torso erect and your head straight, instead of slightly bent, could reduce the wear and tear on your spine dramatically.

More common causes of discomfort are headaches and eye-strain, and providing the right kind and amount of light will certainly help to counteract any problems of this kind (see Lighting). When you're working out your floor plan, it's always helpful if you can position your work surface near a window, especially if it offers an alluring view. You may find, however, that placing your chair so it faces straight into the glare of the morning sun is not ideal. In any case, computers should always be lit from above, or from the side, since illumination shining right onto the screen, or into the user's eyes, will produce a damaging degree of glare.

Finally, one hazard that is often overlooked is the unavoidable number of flexes (cords) and plugs that can be found in a modern, well-equipped work area; you only need a telephone, an answering machine, a computer and a desk light to create a potentially treacherous tangle of trailing wires and overload a single power outlet. By far the safest and most convenient way to solve this problem is by having additional power points fitted near all the equipment that you currently use, or hope to acquire in the future. If this isn't possible, gather the offending flexes (cords) into a wooden or plastic casing, or anchor them to the wall or the underside of a desk or table. This simple measure might help to prevent a serious accident.

Taking precautions

No matter how conscientiously you adhere to safety regulations, and follow the recommended guidelines, however, accidental fires are always a risk; if you are not equipped to cope with them, you are putting your home, your livelihood and your life in jeopardy.

Craftspeople who work with a naked flame or special heat-producing tools tend to be more aware of this hazard than those with administrative jobs, yet ordinary items of office equipment like computers and fax machines (plus, of course, electric kettles and coffee-makers) can be extremely dangerous when their wiring is frayed or their connections faulty. Smoking, too, is another major fire hazard, especially in offices, which are full of flammable materials such as paper.

SPACE CRAFT

With a little resourcefulness, you can squeeze a perfectly serviceable work surface into a surprisingly small area.

One useful trick is to invest in a classic trestle table, which can be dismantled instantly if you want to reclaim the space it occupies. Tucked under the slight overhang of this sleeping gallery (far left) is a pair of wooden trestles topped with a lipped surface that is unusually shallow, so it doesn't impede the flow of traffic.

Specially cut to fit a particularly awkward corner (left), a triangle of pale wood provides an ideal desk for occasional use. Supported by matching battens fixed to the wall, this arrangement leaves the restricted floor area completely clear, and therefore takes up very little visual space. In addition, it enables a wasted recess to be transformed into a valuable work and storage area.

The first and simplest defence against fire is a smoke alarm; widely available and inexpensive to buy, these devices work by producing a piercing wail at the first sign of smoke. Most domestic alarms are powered by small batteries, and they are designed to bleep intermittently when these need replacing. Since warm air, and thus smoke, rises, you should fix your alarm on the ceiling, or high up on a convenient wall.

If you decide to have a fire extinguisher in your office, make sure that it is designed to cope with electrical fires as well as those caused by wood, paper and flammable liquids. Never attempt to use an extinguisher on any electrical equipment, however, before turning the electricity off at the mains first.

Creating a work station that is safe, comfortable and easy to use (right) is one of the most important aspects of working at home full-time.

For less pressing requirements, surprisingly restricted areas can often be exploited successfully. Tucked beneath a sloping roof, for example, a long fitted surface caters for two separate activities (below right). If it's big enough, an under-stairs corner can accommodate a free-standing desk and storage unit. In this one (below left), open treads increase the feeling of light and space.

SETTING UP A WORK STATION

- Provide a work surface that is high enough so that you don't have to bend over it, with plenty of clearance underneath. This will probably be in the region of 63–76cm (25–30in) from the floor.

- Check that there is enough room to accommodate the full range of movements involved in using everyday tools and equipment.

- Position a computer screen at, or just below, eye level. If necessary, support it on a platform of seldom-used books.

- Place the keyboard at lap level. This should be 5–6cm (2–2¼in) below the work surface so that your forearms and wrists fall in a straight horizontal plane when you are typing.

- If your work involves copying written material, avoid placing it flat on an adjoining surface. Instead, anchor it in a vertical position with a document holder placed between the keyboard and the screen, or next to the screen.

- Make sure your feet reach the floor. If they don't, or if you find it more comfortable to work with your legs slightly raised, consider using a foot rest or bar.

Computers should be positioned so that light – natural and artificial – falls on them from the side instead of shining into the operator's eyes, or onto the screen, causing glare (above).

This quiet landing makes an ideal home office (left). The fitted work surface not only maximizes the available space, it is also fixed at the best height for its occupant. In front, a sculptural chair echoes the ceiling's dramatic planes, while sturdy storage cubes lie low to avoid interrupting them.

CABINET WORK

One way of incorporating a practical work and storage area into a spare, minimalist scheme is by investing in a self-contained unit that contains all the necessary facilities within a sleek, stylish cabinet that allows you to shut off your work in progress at the end of the day. Alternatively, commission one from a specialist craftsperson; although this is a more expensive option, the finished piece of furniture would be superbly made, it would fulfil all your needs perfectly and it may even increase in value to become an antique of the future.

INTERIOR ANGLES

The pure geometric form of this armoire-style cabinet (far left) suits the subtle, understated elegance of its surroundings perfectly. In addition, the pale, fine-grain wood chosen for its construction blends skilfully with the plain creamy walls and the natural coir flooring to ensure that its imposing proportions do not dominate the room.

To provide dramatic contrast, the interior is largely constructed from dark-stained wood (left). As well as a bespoke storage system made up of shelves, cupboards and drawers, it is also fitted with a slim flap-down work surface; when files and paperwork pile up, the general-purpose table nearby can also be pressed into service.

Some of the cabinet's internal doors conceal purpose-designed storage compartments for things like stationery, writing materials and a matching set of exquisite linen-covered box files (right).

STYLE

When you're embarking on a freelance
career for the first time, or beginning to
explore a new craft or hobby in earnest,
you may not place the appearance of
your work space very high on your list
of priorities.

An attractive environment, however,
and one that reflects your own personal
tastes and interests, will repay any
modest investment of time and money
by lifting your spirits, increasing your
confidence and enhancing your
enjoyment of any task you undertake.

THE RIGHT LOOK

To provide the best possible atmosphere, all work spaces, no matter where they're located, should be appealing and personal, yet never fussy or distracting. They should be functional and efficient without being institutional and grey, and they should stimulate your energy and creativity, while at the same time providing a tranquil and secure professional base.

An office, workshop or studio that is part of a domestic environment, however, should also have some visual sympathy with the rest of the house. If your work space forms part of a larger area like a bedroom, dining room or living room, this link is particularly important, but establishing it is not so much a matter of covering your desk with a chintzy cloth or attempting to read by the light of a candle-effect table lamp. It is more to do with choosing, where possible, equipment, fittings and accessories that are not only practical, but also complement their surroundings most appropriately; shelves made from natural timber, or painted to match the walls, for example, would blend effortlessly into a traditional room, whereas those made from shiny white laminate are likely to jar. In the same way, a large square of hemmed fabric (plain black in a graphic modern scheme, perhaps, or pastel-hued in a country one)

will protect your computer from dust just as effectively as an institutional grey plastic cover.

Although it is less important for separate, self-contained work spaces to coordinate with the general design scheme, they should still have a style that is broadly in keeping with that of the other rooms. If your house has a high-Victorian feel, for example, an extremely stark, clinical office will sit uncomfortably in the middle of it. If you want to mix antique and modern items, avoid stylistic chaos by combining your chosen elements carefully; black accessories, for example, would live happily with the solid shapes of early oak furniture, but ruin the delicate form of a Georgian desk or cabinet. Whichever style you choose, one immutable rule is to keep your decorating scheme fairly simple. Most occupations or activities, especially if they're carried on full-time, throw up a constant and sometimes uncontrollable jumble of litter and mess. The last thing you need is to increase this visual clutter by adding busily patterned fabric and wallpaper, or elaborate detailing in the form of stencilled borders or tasselled fringes.

When it comes to the main design elements – walls, windows and floors – solid colours are usually best. For

DISPLAY OR DISGUISE

Every activity, domestic or commercial, involves a collection of tools, equipment and materials. Whether you decide to leave these on display, or put them away out of sight, will depend on both the style of your room, and the nature of the items to be stored.

In this kitchen corner (far left), paperwork is kept in accessible storage boxes on open shelves next to linen, crockery and provisions, while remaining within reach of the ad hoc desk.

The owner of this cool, stylish office (left) has taken the opposite approach; strips of grey-washed board are used not only to cover the walls and ceiling, but also to construct an extensive system of fitted drawers and cupboards. Timber-clad (wood-clad) walls offer several practical advantages: they provide effective insulation and hide ugly plaster, pipework or wallpaper.

The line between display and disguise is sometimes blurred. This stunning office (previous page, left) is furnished with objects that would not look out of place in a gallery of modern art. Similarly, this curved desk with its massive pedestal has the same sculptural quality as the vases around it (previous page, right).

■ 33

walls, a painted surface, either plain or subtly colour-washed, is not only the ideal choice, it is also likely to be the cheapest and the easiest to achieve. To create a harmonious, visually uninterrupted background, paint your ceiling to match the walls, and avoid setting up dramatic colour contrasts with your choice of window and floor coverings. This all-over treatment also helps to create an illusion of space, a huge advantage when your work area has been squeezed into a tiny loft or box-room.

Window treatments, too, should aim to convey a business-like impression; for curtains, choose a simple track or rail, a neat heading and, if necessary, a straight pelmet – frills and swags are best employed elsewhere. Similarly, blinds are least appropriate in their fussy festoon or

PERIOD PIECES

In times past, the homes of most prosperous families had a tailor-made office in the form of a separate study or library – a book-lined sanctuary furnished with over-stuffed chairs and a leather-topped desk. While few modern households enjoy the same luxury, the concept is still appealing, and reasonably adaptable.

A vast collection of books sets a similar period style for two living rooms, both of which include a traditional desk among their furnishings (right and left, above). While neither arrangement provides facilities that would support a small business, both rooms offer enough warmth and comfort to take the sting out of paying bills.

Despite its similarly authentic Victorian look, this lofty, light-filled room (left, below) accommodates a fully equipped artist's studio; here, the painter's supplies and materials – easel, brushes, tubes of colour and still-life arrangements – are just as decorative as the conventional furnishings.

Austrian versions. Both vertical louvres and grey metal Venetian blinds are best suited to commercial buildings, but plain roller or Roman designs are reliably adaptable and stylish, and wooden Venetian blinds, especially those with glowing cedar slats, offer a seductive combination of brisk efficiency and high-class good looks.

The most important factor in deciding on a floor covering for your work space is the type of activity you intend to carry on there. On the whole, it's a good idea to avoid thick-pile carpet, since it will wear quickly and unattractively in areas of heavy use, such as under your desk. In the same way, small rugs have an irritating tendency to get caught up in castors or chair legs. For most desk-bound occupations, fitted flat-pile carpet in a durable contract grade is a sound choice, since it provides warmth and softness underfoot as well as aesthetic appeal. If your pursuit is practical rather than clerical, however, a hard floor may be the only sensible option; even when you aren't dabbling in really messy substances like paint or glue, you'll find it much easier to sweep up litter such as pins or tiny screws from cork, vinyl, linoleum or quarry tiles than to vacuum them out of a carpet, no matter how flat.

Colour magic

Colour is probably the single most powerful design element at your disposal, and one whose sphere of influence goes far beyond aesthetics. The right hue used on the walls and ceiling can not only alter a room's apparent size, temperature and brightness, it can even affect the mood of its occupants.

Make these properties work for you by assessing your work space, and your work habits, then selecting a

A PATCH OF COLOUR

Once you've selected one or two basic hues, think carefully about how their intensity will affect you. People whose working environment is dominated by acres of white paper might benefit hugely from an injection of bold azure or rich russet. Conversely, those whose job is directly involved with colour may find that the materials they use every day, such as brightly patterned fabrics or brilliant oil paints, provide more than enough visual stimulation; when this is the case, walls painted in a pale or neutral shade are the best choice.

In this spacious and sunny needlework studio, all the surfaces – walls, pitched ceiling, beams, floor and built-in storage unit – have been painted pure white to keep the quilter's eye fresh, and provide a background that won't compete with the multi-hued textiles on display.

■ 37

WHITE WAYS

Flooded with light and dominated by a stunning view, this seaside study has a fresh, nautical feel that is enhanced by the wooden flooring and the wide expanses of brilliant white used on the walls, the woodwork and the windows.

Beware, however, of falling back on white when your colour confidence deserts you. Far from being a safe and dependable choice, pure white can be very tricky to use successfully on large surfaces such as walls, especially in countries where sunlight tends to be scarce and watery. Too often, white walls look grey and dingy rather than light and clean, so think about using a subtle off-white or cream, or even a warm pastel shade instead.

FUNCTION WITH FLAIR

A sure eye for style and colour and a natural facility with paint have helped the freelance writer who lives here to create a strongly individual work area that fulfils its practical functions in a number of surprising ways.

Fitted with an internal frame and runners, for example, an antique blanket chest takes the place of a conventional filing cabinet. Supplies of paper and small items of stationery are kept in a reproduction tallboy (highboy) that has been given a distressed finish to match the painted chest. The table lamp, embellished with calligraphy motifs, provides subtle background illumination as well as a witty visual reference to its owner's vocation. Another repro find, the graceful table harmonizes perfectly with the rest of the room and provides a generous work surface.

suitable main colour. Remember, though, that in some cases, physical considerations are less important than psychological ones; as long as your room looks appropriate and appealing, there is little to be gained by making it seem slightly larger than it really is. But if you spend all day negotiating prices, doing deals and generally feeling stressed, creating a relaxing atmosphere should be given a high priority. If, on the other hand, working on your own for long hours produces drowsiness and lack of concentration, a cheerful, invigorating scheme might make a real difference.

On display

In many work areas, every wall and surface is crammed with heavily laden shelves, piles of paper, and the equipment and materials in constant use. In rooms like this, objects set out solely for display or pictures hung on the wall frequently take up valuable space and add to the general impression of disorder.

If you do have a wall or a corner that could use brightening up, however, explore the decorative potential of the objects that are an intrinsic part of what you do. Instead of hiding away skeins of coloured wool, say, pile them into a row of huge glass storage jars. Fix a series of tiny shelves to set off ranks of jewel-hued sewing threads; these will not only look striking, they will also remain free of the irritating tangles that result from flinging them in a drawer or a basket. If you work with textiles, suspend a large square of fabric from a wooden, brass or cane pole. Alternatively, compose an arrangement of exquisitely crafted tools to hang above a work bench, or frame a selection of your favourite covers from a trade journal.

With its walls covered from picture to dado rail (plate to chair rail) in rows of monochrome images, this bright white studio (right) is a contemporary interpretation of an eighteenth-century print room. In the original version, the prints would have been pasted down, linked together with stencilled garlands or ropes, then varnished. Here, each print is tacked loosely in position so the walls can act as a constantly changing portfolio of the artist's work.

SQUARING UP

The strong geometric form of this grid-shaped storage system dominates the dual-purpose living/work area and imposes a sense of visual order and discipline on a wildly eclectic assortment of books, pictures, artefacts, files and office impedimenta.

Tucked discreetly behind the vast marble desk is a Harry Bertoia side chair; designed in 1951, this classic of the international modern furnishing style is constructed from chrome wire welded into a strong lattice structure that echoes the room's graphic theme. This theme is further reinforced by the high sash window that has been picked out in black and left free of curtains or blinds.

COLOUR CODES

- A room decorated with warm tones such as rose, ochre or apricot can actually increase the body temperature of its occupants slightly, whereas the same area painted in cool shades of blue or mauve will have the opposite effect.

- Dark colours absorb more light than pale ones, so the same amount of illumination will be less effective in a terracotta room than in a cream one.

- Light colours open out a room and make it seem larger; deeper ones produce a more enclosed feeling.

- Soft tints such as peach, pastel pink and pale green are known for their calming influence, while vivid ones like orange and sunshine yellow have a stimulating effect.

- Colours are strongly affected by light. Cool blues and greens, therefore, are often more successful in sunny, south-facing rooms than in those with a north-facing aspect, where the light is cold all day.

- A scheme consisting of several bright, clashing hues would be distracting to work in, so if you harbour a wild colour fantasy, indulge it in an area that is occupied for limited periods only, such as a dining room.

ADAPTABLE DECO

One historical decorative style that offers a perfect combination of comfort, elegance and efficiency is Art Deco. Born during the post-war era of the 1920s, this was the first international movement to reflect the modern view that good design must go hand in hand with practicality.

The ingenious item of DIY office furniture used here was assembled from two quintessential Art Deco storage cabinets; bridging them with a slab of thick wood has produced a roomy and functional desk with six drawers in each of its two pedestals, plus a shallow cupboard at each end.

On the floor, plain polished boards blend effortlessly into the scheme, and require much less maintenance than loose rugs or a fitted carpet.

COLONIAL CHARM

This quiet correspondence corner exudes charm and simplicity, and is typical of the graceful Shaker style that inspired it. The defining characteristics of this popular eighteenth-century design idiom – simplicity, fitness for purpose and fine craftsmanship – make it ideally suited to work spaces of any kind.

Here, plain buff walls are relieved only by bare wooden beams and a painted peg rail fixed at picture (plate) rail height, which could be adapted to cater for a wide variety of storage needs. Fitted with a full-width drawer, the homely desk is big enough to accommodate a selection of stationery organized in baskets and trays made from natural wicker and wood.

Suspended between the ceiling beams, a modern rise-and-fall pendant light adds the convenience of modern technology without compromising the style's integrity.

STORAGE

A well-planned storage system can transform your working life. Not only will it take up far less room than a collection of casual, haphazard arrangements, it will also ensure that all your equipment remains organized, safe and easily accessible.

Furthermore, a tidy, disciplined environment produces a feeling of professional calm, confidence and control that helps you keep a cool head when things go wrong and the pressure begins to mount.

A PLACE FOR EVERYTHING

No work space can function effectively without a well-planned storage system. Getting this element right will go a long way towards eliminating untidiness, maximizing available space and increasing productivity by making every piece of paper, or item of equipment or material, easily accessible. Also, a neat, ordered supply cupboard will alert you immediately when stocks are running low.

Listing everything that your work space will be expected to accommodate (see page 14) should give you a fair idea of your storage requirements. Chosen with stylistic flair and

a little common sense, the furnishings and accessories you select to cope with them can even become decorative features in their own right.

Shelf life

One furnishing item that forms a vital part of most work spaces is shelving, either built-in, or in the form of free-standing units. At the planning and selecting stage, your first priority should be to make sure the capacity you provide is adequate. To do this, allow enough room for

Almost every room, however small or awkwardly shaped, can provide greater capacity for storage than a quick glance would suggest.

In this open-plan warehouse (loft) conversion (right), the flight of polished wooden steps that leads from the book-lined study to the mezzanine bedroom above does double duty as a capacious drawer unit.

The steeply sloping ceiling of this sunny attic studio (left) restricts the arrangement of free-standing furniture, but built-in shelves make full use of the wall space available.

A wide, deep alcove offers maximum flexibility for planning an extensive built-in run of shelves and a large work surface (previous page, left). When the architecture of your room does not supply a natural alcove, however, create one yourself by buying or constructing a ceiling-height run of spacious cupboards (previous page, right).

TREASURES FROM THE PAST

Auction rooms and specialist second-hand dealers are an excellent source of low-cost office equipment of all kinds, especially when your budget is tight. In addition, outlets like these are the only potential source for a number of stylish and functional items that are ideal for domestic work spaces, but were either never mass produced, or are no longer widely available. Look out for:

■ old-fashioned shop fittings, such as shelf units and storage and display cabinets, some of which have useful cupboards and drawers as well

■ filing cabinets, designed in the standard way with deep drawers but made in wood with brass detailing

■ traditional wooden desks, or – if you need a larger surface – scrubbed, farmhouse-sized kitchen tables with wide drawers

■ storage boxes, made either from tin, wood (look for empty cutlery canteens or small pine chests that were originally portable safes) or sturdy card; old hat boxes would be ideal for needlework supplies

■ wooden filing trays and stationery racks, which, like the larger cabinets, often have solid brass trim

such things as books and box files, then add an extra 25–50 per cent for the inevitable forgotten extras and the additional things you will acquire as times goes by.

Fitted shelves use space most efficiently, and are often the cheapest option. It's important, however, to make them sturdy and ensure they have plenty of support, since there are few sights as uninspiring as a row of thin shelves sagging under the weight of their contents. If yours are strong but skinny, make them look more solid by fixing a strip of wide edging (wood or laminate) to the front of each one. The main disadvantage of built-in shelves is that they are cumbersome to remove and re-build should you decide to set up in another room, or move to a new house.

For maximum flexibility, consider free-standing shelves of some kind; if your requirements are modest, you may

WAYS WITH WALLS

A spare patch of wall can easily be
adapted to meet the requirements of
a variety of different storage needs.

A previous owner of this period
property (right) filled a shallow recess
in the dining room with fitted cupboards
and drawers for crockery, cutlery and
linen. To take advantage of these
existing storage facilities, the home-
based architect who now lives here has
set up her drawing board nearby.

In this sleek, modern work space
(left), another architect keeps large
technical drawings safe and accessible
by rolling them up and slotting them into
a row of wall-fixed hooks.

Behind a pair of full-height sliding
doors, a shallow built-in shelf unit
swallows up office clutter so the pure
geometric form of the triangular desk
can remain unsullied (far left). For the
same reason, the jointed desk lamp was
wired directly into an adjacent wall.

SECTIONAL STORAGE

Acquired in single units, then added to
and rearranged according to budget and
circumstances, this sectional storage
system fulfils two important functions:
it holds a vast number of books, files
magazines and small items of office
equipment, and it divides the room into
two separate work areas.

Free-standing shelf units like
these are not only infinitely flexible
in arrangement, they can also be
dismantled and reassembled fairly easily
in a new location. When they are stacked
as high as this, though, and packed with
heavy objects, it might be wise to anchor
the ones at the top to the wall with a
couple of long screws.

FLYING COLOURS

When the materials you use every day are beautiful in their own right, it's a shame to hide them away. Crammed full of richly coloured tapestry wools, this ingenious wall-mounted storage rack (right) makes a bold, graphic display and accommodates a wide variety of shades and weights, both in its triangular- and diamond-shaped compartments, and along the shelf at the top.

Constructed from lengths of inexpensive softwood, this unit also acts as an informal pinboard for postcards, photographs, fabric swatches and any other sources of inspiration.

even get by with a domestic bookcase, which could be anything from a valuable antique to a basic, self-assembly model made from MDF (medium-density fibreboard).

Hidden assets

For large or awkwardly shaped objects that would look unsightly on open shelves, search out some form of concealed storage. Designers' plan chests (flat files), for example, with their huge, shallow drawers, are ideal not only for storing large sheets of paper or card, but also for keeping any collection of smallish objects – such as hand-painted plates – accessible and free of dust. In addition, they also have a roomy surface area that might be ideal for a fax machine or a small photocopier.

Commercial filing cabinets have particularly deep drawers that can accommodate many things other than hanging files. Often, though, an ordinary domestic chest of drawers is a better choice for concealed storage, since these are available in a much wider range of sizes, and their

design often includes drawers of several different widths and depths that offer a considerable degree of flexibility. For very large, or seldom-used, articles, a blanket box, steamer trunk or wicker chest might offer the solution; particularly strong models can even double up as extra seating in an emergency.

File away

If your occupation involves constant referral to a large number of files, it's hard to improve on the design of the traditional filing cabinet, widely available in two-, three- or four-drawer versions. (A single four-drawer model provides maximum capacity for minimum floor space, while two two-drawer cabinets placed side by side hold the same amount, and also provide a useful surface for a printer or even tea-making equipment.) The grey metal version of this classic is probably the most familiar, but office-equipment suppliers often sell them in white and a small range of colours as well. If you can't find the colour you want, or if your budget is limited, look for an undamaged second-hand model and transform it with enamel spray paint, which is available in an enormous range of shades.

It may be, of course, that your files are not nearly extensive enough to fill even a two-drawer cabinet. In this case, either box files or ring binders would probably be most suitable. When you have little need to refer to paperwork once it's filed away, neat, easy-to-store box files are ideal; if yours are on display, you might prefer coloured or patterned designs to conventional plain ones. If you regularly refer to your files, however, you might tire of burrowing through the layers of paper in a box file, and prefer to use ring binders with coloured index tabs instead.

Alternatively, many large wooden fruit or wine crates are exactly the right shape to hold folding wallet files of foolscap (legal) size; if your system is small and simple, the whole lot might fit neatly into a single crate.

Bits and pieces

Work spaces that cater for handicrafts and hobbies are likely to be littered with tools and materials. In a sewing room, for example, you will have to store not only a sewing machine, ironing board and fabric, but also a wide range of accessories. What you need is a system that makes everything easy to see and reach. Small, frequently used items – in this case things like pins, needles, scissors and thimbles – are best kept together, ideally in a basket or box divided internally so the contents don't get mixed up or damaged. Larger objects such as paper patterns, or small items that tend to be stored in quantity, like threads and buttons, might suit a collection of coordinating boxes, each one a different size or colour to avoid confusion; you can find these in a stationery shop or the haberdashery (notions) section of a department store. Alternatively, invest in a range of clear plastic containers, which reveal the nature and quantity of their contents at a glance. Another practical repository for office or craft supplies is a

Free-standing shelving units designed for industrial or commercial purposes have much to recommend them: they have a straightforward, professional look, they offer extensive storage capacity and they are extremely strong. To suit a traditional scheme, look for wooden shelves designed for the retail trade. For a more contemporary look, choose one of the metal systems, which consist of shelves and uprights of various sizes that bolt together like a giant building set.

Assembled on an almost factory-sized scale, these basic metal shelves (right) have been carefully spaced so they can accommodate everything from tall books to flat boxes and files. The same construction principle, however, meets more modest storage needs just as effectively. In this well-planned office (left), a small industrial storage unit supplements two long shelves that have been cleverly designed to have no visible means of support.

drawer unit from a cube storage system. Generally made from plastic or wood, these measure only about 38cm (15in) square, and so can easily fit on a shelf or a desk.

To provide larger-scale storage of this kind, install a classic industrial system consisting of a wall-fixed metal rack onto which you slot plastic storage bins of various sizes and colours. Or make use of the available wall space by installing a large pegboard or wire grid onto which you can either slot a range of specially designed baskets, or hang suitable items directly. Even an ordinary pinboard can provide useful storage space for things like keys, colour swatches and invoices fastened together with a bulldog clip, as well as a convenient display area for often-used information like telephone numbers and tax codes.

On the surface

Most people involved in essentially paperwork-based jobs find it easier to work at a surface that is organized in some way. Frustrating, time-wasting piles of letters and files, for example, become manageable when they are sorted into a row of filing baskets. As well as the plastic and wire ones available in office-supply shops (look, too, for wire baskets that clip on under a shelf), consider those made of wood or

wicker, both of which have a warmer, more traditional look. Or choose several in different colours so that their contents can be instantly identified.

If drawer space is limited, organize small stationery items into a stylish basket that sits on top of your desk; those who prefer a more graphic look could use a square metal cake tin in the same way (a large rectangular one – available from a catering supply company – would be ideal for filing). Similarly, stand pens and pencils in a pretty jug, a small vase, an olive-oil tin or a clear laboratory beaker, and keep paper clips in a demi-tasse cup or a Petri dish.

Depending on their contents, fit one or two desk drawers with a divided stationery rack, and use the time-honoured trick of installing a plastic, wooden or wicker cutlery tray in the top one to hold the chaos at bay.

The storage arrangements you choose should suit their contents as well as their surroundings.

The owner of this very traditional home office (left) has tucked a mountain of seldom-used files well out of the way in an old cabinet originally designed for bulky legal documents; the enormous wooden desk has nine drawers that provide plenty of concealed storage facilities for paperwork and equipment in use on a daily basis.

In complete contrast, a rough wooden box divided into deep, cube-shaped cubbyholes (far left) makes an ideal container for the vast collection of pens, pencils, tubes, brushes and markers that threaten to overrun the work surface of anyone involved in painting, drawing or graphic design.

CARVED WITH PRIDE

To make sure sharp or pointed
implements remain in good condition,
and to guard against injuries, avoid
storing them loose in a drawer or chest.

The simple wooden rack fixed right
above this wood carver's bench keeps
frequently used tools out of harm's way
and within easy reach (left). At the same
time, it shows off their bright colours
and satisfying shapes. The small shelves
and drawers under the work surface hold
reference material, rough drawings and
a collection of paints and wood stains.

METAL WORK

The most useful storage solution for
bulky, heavy or awkwardly shaped items
is often a collection of big, strong
metal boxes.

   Neatly stacked on a tall, slim storage
tower (below) are an assortment of
these containers at their most
sophisticated, with a smooth, shiny

finish, gracefully rounded corners and
neatly fitting lids.

   Equally practical, but rather more
rough-and-ready in style, this set of
open-topped metal crates with strong
carrying handles (right) affords instant
access to their contents.

BRIGHT BEADS

An ideal candidate for the bold display school of storage solutions, tiny glass beads would in any case be a nightmare to sort out if they accidentally got mixed up. On these purpose-built shelves (right, above), beads have been set out in clear glass containers that keep them safe and orderly, yet reveal their appealing colours and shapes.

On the work surface below, finished bracelets and necklaces are stored in the large, thick glass jars normally used for bottling fruit and vegetables.

CONCEALED COMPARTMENTS

Whatever their function, all work spaces should include some provision for everyday clutter to be hidden away out of sight.

Below the thick stone work bench in this charming potting shed (left, above), a row of deep wooden drawers, clearly and elegantly labelled with their contents, fulfils this function perfectly.

A completely different, but equally effective, solution has been employed in this very feminine correspondence corner (left, below). Here, a hinged shelf unit swings out from under the work surface to reveal a useful assortment of small stationery items.

EQUIPMENT

One of the most important aspects of setting up an efficient work space is selecting the most suitable equipment for the tasks at hand. From relatively simple things like chairs and desks, however, to the most complex pieces of specialist machinery, the range of choice available can often seem bewildering, and the cost of making mistakes cripplingly high. Before you make any decisions, therefore, it's a good idea to assess your needs carefully and consider all the options available.

TRADE TOOLS

Whatever your occupation or activity, its most basic requirements are a surface to work at and a chair to sit on. Otherwise, the amount and the type of equipment you require will vary enormously according to the nature of the task and your degree of commitment to it in terms of time, money and enthusiasm.

Surface values

Although some specialist crafts and hobbies require a sophisticated facility like an easel, a loom or a workbench, most home-based jobs are likely to be carried out at some

A built-in work surface often provides more space than a conventional desk, and it can be fixed at whatever height you choose. What's more, this arrangement allows you to add storage pedestals that suit your needs precisely: shallow drawers for pens and stationery, deep ones for hanging files, or a combination of the two. Some are even available with castors so you can move them around easily.

On this L-shaped surface (right), an ingenious computer stand raises the screen to eye level, and contains a pull-out drawer so the keyboard can be tucked away out of sight when it's not required.

CLEAR THE DECKS

If you don't need to use your typewriter or computer all the time, try to position your keyboard so it doesn't clutter up your main work surface. Here, a typewriter trolley, correctly designed to be slightly lower than desk height, swings into position as needed (left).

An alternative, but less compact, solution is to provide a second surface elsewhere in the room. A short distance from the built-in work space illustrated on page 11, a full-sized dining table accommodates a large-screen computer, plus its keyboard, mouse and printer (previous page, left).

The artist who owns this tiny studio (previous page, right), has conserved precious surface area by squeezing his huge collection of brushes into an eclectic assortment of colourful tins, pots and buckets.

BARE NECESSITIES

This functional home office has been
designed around a custom-made work
top, anchored in position with wall-fixed
battens instead of legs or trestles. To
keep costs down, a lightweight wooden
basket takes the place of a standard
waste-paper bin, while documents and
files are stored in wooden fruit and
vegetable crates. On the work surface,
small stationery items are concealed in
inexpensive metal canisters more usually
seen in the kitchen.

Higher than a standard office model,
the sturdy workbench chair has a seat
that can be raised or lowered by turning
it like a screw head.

WINNING SEATS

The chairs specified by the designer of this luxuriously appointed office (left) have a classic look that would suit a small home work space just as well. Although they are not the cheapest models on the market, their fully adjustable seat and back, stable base and comfortable arm rests make them ideally suited to their purpose, and well worth investing in.

For hiding away messy work-in-progress, it's hard to beat the design of a traditional wooden roll-top desk. In this informal study corner (right) the nostalgic style is reinforced by a classic bentwood chair.

People who suffer from low-back pain often find the conventional sitting posture uncomfortable, especially over long periods. When this is the case, many experts recommend some kind of forward-tilt seating to reduce pressure on the lumbar spine. One of the most popular forms of this healthy alternative is a kneeler chair like the one that fits so comfortably into this restrained Japanese interior (far right).

sort of desk. The most expensive and sophisticated models are like miniature work stations in themselves, with a complex L or U shape and built-in extras such as extending pedestal units and privacy screens. Most people, however, can manage perfectly well with something simpler: a basic commercial desk, either new or second hand, a small but sturdy dining or trestle table, or just a deep, wide built-in shelf. Those who prefer performing some tasks at an angled surface may want to invest in a portable drawing board that can be stored elsewhere when it's not in use.

The most important considerations to bear in mind are surface area and height; purpose-designed desks are likely to be suitable (the top-quality ones have a height-adjustment mechanism), but if you intend to adapt an ordinary table, check that it's at least approximately the right height; you can compensate for one that is very slightly too high or too low with an adjustable chair.

Seating plans

Your chair should be chosen according to the amount of time you intend to spend in it. If your lengthiest task is likely to be recording each day's events in your diary, you can choose your seating purely on the basis of appearance or availability. If, however, you will be working for long periods of time, it's vital that you invest in a good-quality, ergonomically designed chair that will not only provide maximum comfort, but also prevent strain and possibly permanent damage to your back, neck and shoulders.

FULL- OR PART-TIME

To accommodate a craft or a hobby that you pursue only occasionally, choose furnishings that can be folded up and stored away to free the floor area for other things. In this wood-clad attic conversion (left, above), a vast wooden work surface sits firmly on a pair of trestles, and seating for two takes the form of a pair of Plia chairs that are almost flat in their collapsed state.

For more permanent quarters, one particularly appealing form of seating is an old-fashioned wooden office chair (left, below). With its curved, slatted back and strong arms, this relic from a past age instantly creates a feeling of security and nostalgia.

Screen play

In the past few years, computers have become as familiar and as unthreatening as video recorders or CD players. Huge numbers of home-based businesses are completely focused around a keyboard and a screen, and many more rely on a computer for administrative tasks such as invoicing, accounting and correspondence.

In their wake, however, these sophisticated machines have brought a new, and potentially serious, work-place health hazard in the form of repetitive strain injury, or RSI. In the dark ages, typing on a manual machine was a positively healthy activity, since the pressure required to depress the keys built up strength in the muscles and

Try clearing your desk of clutter by making full use of walls and windows. Replace your diary, for example, with a giant planner that gets wiped clean at the end of the week, or a row of clips that hold *aides-mémoire* for each day.

Hang up a shiny chrome grid that can be used for both storage and display, or brighten up a boring blind by festooning the edges with postcards.

tendons involved. Even with electric typewriters, RSI was rare, because operating them still required a wide range of movements: returning the carriage, replacing the paper, painting out errors and so on. On a computer, however, there is almost no variety of movement, and the keys are so sensitive that their operation requires only the lightest pressure and tiniest movement. Because of this, they cannot bear the weight of resting fingers, so the muscles in the wrists, hands and fingers, while never exercised enough to strengthen them, are held in a state of slight but constant tension for extended periods, and it's this tension that leads to RSI. To lower your risk, look for a keyboard with strongly sprung keys that will exercise your fingers,

and allow you to rest them occasionally in position. The keyboard should be almost flat, or with a very slight angle, so your wrists and hands form a straight line when you work. It's also important that the keyboard is detachable from the screen, so it can be positioned for maximum comfort and safety.

One accessory that is designed to guard against RSI is a wrist support, a flat bar with adjustable height and angle that you place in front of your keyboard. Opinion on its effectiveness, however, is sharply divided; some people wouldn't work without one, while others claim they make the problem worse by impeding circulation and supporting the wrists at an undesirable angle.

CHAIR CHECKLIST

A well-designed chair provides good support and allows maximum ease of movement, making it possible for you to work for long periods without feeling uncomfortable, or placing undue strain on any part of your body. A good chair should have:

- A padded back that is adjustable both in height and in angle so that it will support the lumbar spine (low back), a very common area of weakness and pain.

- A padded seat that can be moved up or down to suit your height and the height of the desk. Ideally, you should be able to sit with your thighs parallel to the floor and your feet flat, or on a foot rest.

- A stable base: the best-designed models have five legs.

- A swivel mechanism so you can shift your focus and position without twisting your neck and back.

- Padded arm rests are an optional extra. Many people find them extremely comfortable, especially when they're adjustable in height, but it's important to make sure they don't prevent your chair from being positioned sufficiently close to the work surface.

The machine maze

For people with a lot of money and a passion for high-tech toys, the home office is a potential fantasy playground, with scope for the use of a multi-feature telephone, an answering machine, a photocopier, a facsimile machine and even more esoteric gadgets like portable shredders.

Before you decide to invest in any one of these, however, look carefully at all the available brands and models, then examine each one against your needs and your budget. In this way, you won't miss out on a service or a feature that would be of great help, or waste money on a range of options you will never use.

One obvious way to save both money and space is by choosing machines that combine two or more functions in one, like a fax/answering machine, or even a telephone/fax/answering machine. The principle is a sound one, but with multi-function appliances, it's even more vital to investigate the comparative research thoroughly, and invest in the highest-quality product you can afford. Otherwise, you could end up with an inferior contraption that performs none of its functions efficiently. Another major disadvantage of very complicated models is that when one function fails, you have to struggle along without the others while your machine is being repaired.

CREATIVE CRAFTS

An artist's eye and the skill of a master cabinet-maker are both evident in the layout of this efficient and attractive workshop (right). Framed like a priceless painting, a collection of tools is set out in a logical and pleasing arrangement, while bits of carving and moulding hang from the ceiling like stalactites.

The design of many craft studios and work spaces demonstrates a similarly skilful blend of looks and practicality. The fashion designer and dressmaker who works in this large tiled room (left) rescued her huge cutting table from an old department store that was closing down. The tall, glass-fronted display case behind it was salvaged from the haberdashery (notions) department of the same establishment. Undeniably up-to-date, however, is the purpose-designed office chair on which she sits to draft patterns and sketch out new ideas.

LIGHTING

In work areas, even more than in those designed for relaxation, it is important to treat lighting as a basic element in the room's design, rather than just a decorative accessory.

Whatever your activity, choosing the right illumination for your home office or studio will not only make the space a more attractive, comfortable and safer place to work in, it will also help you to focus and sustain your concentration and therefore increase your productivity.

BRIGHT IDEAS

Your work space will benefit from good lighting in a number of ways: it will be easier to work in, and therefore more efficient; it will be comfortable, because poor illumination leads to eye-strain and headaches; it will be more attractive, since the right lighting brings out the best in rooms as well as people, and it will be many times safer than a dimly-lit and potentially dangerous corner.

Fit for purpose

There are two elements involved in a well-planned work-space lighting system: task lighting and background lighting. Task lighting, as its name suggests, provides strong illumination that is centred on your immediate work area. In a multi-purpose room, task lighting can also define a work area visually, and many people who operate from a living room or bedroom find it easier to concentrate when their attention is focused within a circle of brightness.

Background lighting, on the other hand, covers a much wider area. It tends to be considerably more subtle, and its main function is to soften the potentially harsh contrast between the pool of light on your work, and the darkness around it. Furthermore, if your work space is located in an area that doesn't get a great deal of natural light, such as a basement, an attic or a landing, good background lighting will also make it safer by revealing hazards such as a tangle of wiring, a change of floor level or a flight of stairs.

The task at hand

The most effective task lighting usually takes the form of a desk lamp, a spot fitting clipped to a nearby shelf or a

concealed or diffused fluorescent strip fixed above your desk or work table. The best desk lamps and, by definition, all spot fittings, have the advantage of being directional in some way – that is, they rotate, bend or swivel to throw light wherever it's most needed. Among the best-known examples are the standard Anglepoise (jointed) design and the traditional goose-neck model with its heavy base and long bendy stem. Other directional fittings provide movement by means of a sliding arm, a hinged arm or shade, or a moving knuckle joint.

For practicality, value and unpretentious good looks, it's hard to improve on the standard Anglepoise (jointed) desk lamp. Task lighting for this contemporary partners' desk (right) comes from a pair of shiny black models attached to a nearby shelf. Instead of being fixed with sprung clips, however, these have been screwed directly into the wood, then anchored in place on the other side.

In this almost hospital-like living space (left), two pairs of white angled lamps are fixed to the top of a tall screen that acts as a giant headboard, and helps to set off the sleeping area from the adjacent office. Made entirely from glass bricks, the screen admits plenty of natural light to act as background illumination.

When your desk is situated right beside a huge window, the sun provides plenty of good task lighting on fine days. Here (previous page, left), a pair of angled fittings (fixtures) are ready to take over when darkness falls.

Anglepoise (jointed) lamps operate on a system of counter-balances that has inspired many modern versions, like this black model with its heavy base and disc-shaped head (previous page, right).

THREE TIMES LUCKY

Justifying its status as an office classic, the angled desk lamp lends itself to yet another design interpretation in this sophisticated black-and-cream work and living space.

Fixed with miniature G-clamps to a shelf above the sofa are two of these fittings (fixtures). Made from satin-finished aluminium, their almost industrial styling is belied by surprisingly traditional drum-shaped shades. Across the room, providing plenty of illumination for processing paperwork, is a matching desk model with a circular base.

Strip lights are less flexible, but, cleverly concealed under a shelf, they take up no space at all, either physically or visually, and so come into their own in either very restricted spaces, or minimalist design schemes.

Whatever form of task lighting you choose, the illumination it provides should be clear and reasonably neutral – that is without a definite yellow, pink or blue cast. This is especially important if you work in a field like photography or design, where colour plays an important part. In this regard, ordinary tungsten (incandescent) bulbs are slightly superior to fluorescent ones. Above all, the light you provide must be sufficiently strong. Age, too, should be taken into account: an adult of 40 needs three times more light than a child of ten to perform the same task, while someone of 60 requires 15 times more light.

To avoid working in your own shadow, position any directional task lighting on (or above) the opposite side of the work surface from your dominant hand, and far enough away so the light falls across your work diagonally: from the top left, if you're right-handed and vice versa. At the same time, make sure no light shines directly onto a computer screen to cause irritating glare. If the glare on your screen is caused by sunlight from a nearby window, invest in a translucent blind or a sheer curtain, both of which will filter the sun's rays without blocking them out altogether. Those who spend long hours at a screen should also avoid lamps that have a tendency to flicker, since even an imperceptible degree of movement can produce a blinding headache.

If you work with hand tools of any kind, a certain amount of vibration is inevitable, and this can not only cause light emanating from a desk lamp to flicker

Desk lamps that have heads as small as this one (above) provide powerful illumination by means of a tiny tungsten halogen (halogen) bulb. Although these are more expensive to buy than ordinary tungsten (incandescent) light bulbs, they last much longer, and they are marginally more energy efficient.

The compact shape of tungsten halogen (halogen) bulbs, and their accurate colour rendering, make them a popular choice for many of the stylish contemporary fittings (fixtures) favoured by architects and designers.

MAKING LIGHT WORK

Achieving an effective lighting system is much easier when you steer clear of a few common pitfalls.

- In the interest of style, you may be tempted to choose an ordinary table lamp for your work surface, but remember that these fittings (fixtures) are designed essentially to look attractive and to help create a soft, relaxing atmosphere. As a result, they are extremely unlikely to provide adequate task lighting.

- When you are adjusting a directional desk lamp, always make sure the bare bulb is completely concealed, since even a small degree of exposure will produce an irritating level of glare.

- Never depend too heavily on natural light; even if your desk is positioned right in front of a window, you will still need efficient task lighting for backup on gloomy days, and subtle background illumination for when you work at night.

- Avoid fixing a central ceiling light to fulfil any of your requirements. Wherever it appears, this ubiquitous form of lighting manages to be both harsh and ineffectual, and tends to have an unfortunate flattening effect on everything around it.

TOP PRIORITY

If you have to squeeze a work station into a restricted space, keep the surface clear by lighting it from above.

The clamp spotlight shining down on this compact home office (left, above) both rotates and swivels so it can illuminate the computer, the surface or, when the working day is over, the colourful images on the pinboard.

If a clamp fitting is not suitable, consider installing a ceiling-fixed track to which you can attach a whole row of spotlights. In this study (left, below) two slim metal cylinders hold standard reflector spot bulbs, and slide smoothly along their track to throw light wherever it is needed.

On the mellow pine table that constitutes the working corner of this stylish French living room (right), a decorative table lamp casts a warm relaxing glow. When there is work to be done, though, serious illumination comes from a factory-style pendant lamp.

dramatically, it also increases the risk of a top-heavy design toppling over. To solve this problem, provide task lighting in the form of a clamp fitting attached to a nearby shelf, or a swivel spot fixed to an adjacent wall.

In the background

If you are carving your work area out of an existing room, the fittings (fixtures) that are already in place can probably provide all the background illumination you need. In a bedroom, for example, one or two small table lamps will balance your task lighting effectively without adding unnecessary distraction. One accessory that is particularly useful in multi-purpose rooms is a dimmer switch; connected to several table or wall lights in a living room, for example, it will lower their brightness when you're in working mode, then bring it up to full strength when you want to relax on the sofa with the evening paper.

In a single-purpose work room, table lamps are also a sound choice for background lighting; where available surfaces are in short supply, choose an alternative such as a standard lamp, a low-hanging pendant, free-standing uplighters, ceiling or wall-mounted tracks, recessed ceiling spots or downlighters, or special display fittings (fixtures) such as picture lights. Wall lights of every description fulfil this function perfectly, and are available in an enormous variety of designs, from traditional brass models, to simple globes, wall-mounted uplighters and bulkhead fittings (fixtures) intended for use in warehouses and factories. If the pared-down industrial look appeals to you, or if your work space is so large that domestic lighting is inadequate, explore specialist trade suppliers, as well as conventional consumer outlets, for suitable designs.

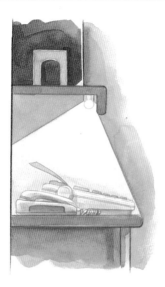

Tucked behind a deep wood edging, a top-fixed fluorescent strip light is completely invisible and takes up very little room (above).

Fluorescent tubes far outlast tungsten (incandescent) bulbs, and they use energy more efficiently, but many give off a cool light that some people find harsh and unflattering.

THE RIGHT DIRECTION

Desk-top lights should be positioned above your work, and slightly to the left if you're right-handed, or vice versa. The owner of this solid glass work surface (left) is right-handed, so placing the swivel-arm lamp in the top left corner of the table ensures clear, shadowless illumination.

When two people – one right- and one left-handed – occupy a single work space at different times, they can either move a single desk lamp back and forth as necessary, or buy two angled lamps and clamp one to each side of the desk (right). Note also the ceiling-recessed spotlight that creates a soft background glow and highlights the pinboard.

INDEX

Page numbers in *italic* refer to illustrations

PUBLISHER'S ACKNOWLEDGMENTS

We would like to thank the following photographers and organizations for their permission to reproduce the photographs in this book:

Front cover: J.C. Buggeai/S.I.P./Elizabeth Whiting & Associates; Back cover: V.T. Wonen/Spaarnestad/Utrecht/Holland; 1 Alexandre Baillache (Designer: Christian Liaigre)/Stylograph; 2 Paul Ryan (Architect: Ian Hay)/Conran Octopus; 3 Alexandre Baillache (Designer: Christian Liaigre)/Stylograph; 4-5 Marie Claire Maison/Nicolas Tosi (Stylist: Catherine Ardouin); 6 Reiner Blunck; 8-9 Nicholas Kane (Architect: Mark Guard Associates)/Arcaid; 9 right Elizabeth Whiting & Associates; 10-11 Paul Ryan (Architect: Ian Hay)/Conran Octopus; 12 John Freeman; 13 David Phelps; 14 Simon Brown (Designer: John Stefanidis)/Interior World; 15 Marie Claire Maison/Gilles de Chabaneix (Stylist: Catherine Ardouin); 16-17 Eigen Huis & Interieur/Spaarnestad/Utrecht/Holland; 18 Paul Ryan/International Interiors; 19 Paul Warchol; 20-21 Tim Street-Porter (Architect: Barton Myers); 22-23 Lars Hallén; 23 Mark Darley/Esto; 24 Richard Paul (Designer: Dominique Vaulthier); 25 Reiner Blunck; 26 left V.T. Wonen/Spaarnestad/Utrecht/Holland; 26 right Elizabeth Whiting & Associates; 27 above Ornella Sancassani; 27 below Jerome Darblay; 28 left Alexandre Baillache (Designer: Christian Liaigre)/Stylograph; 28 right Alexandre Baillache (Designer: Christian Liaigre)/Stylograph; 29 Alexandre Baillache (Designer: Christian Liaigre)/Stylograph; 30-31 Reiner Blunck; 31 right Marie Claire Maison/Jean-Pierre Godeaut (Stylist: J.P. Billaud); 32-33 Richard Bryant (Architect: GEA; Interior Designer: MBA Decoration)/Arcaid; 32 left Christopher Drake/Robert Harding Picture Library; 34 above Guillaume de Laubier/Stylograph; 34 below Christian Sarramon; 35 Simon Brown/Interior World; 36-37 Jerome Darblay (Architect: Roderick James); 38 Ron Sutherland; 39 Country Living/Christopher Drake; 40 Simon Brown/Interior World; 40-41 Christian Sarramon; 42 Christian Sarramon; 43 William Waldron/S.I.P./Elizabeth Whiting & Associates; 44-45 J.C. Buggeai/S.I.P./Elizabeth Whiting & Associates; 45 right Alberto Piovano (Architect: Stickland Coombe Architecture)/Arcaid; 46 Vogue Living/Geoff Lung; 47 Abitare/Leo Torri; 48 left S. Couturier/Archipress; 48 right René Stoeltie; 49 Mark Darley/Esto; 50 Richard Davies; 51 Elizabeth Whiting & Associates; 52 Deidi von Schaewen; 53 Camera Press; 54 left Marie Claire Maison/Antoine Rozès; 54 right Marie Claire Maison/Nicolas Tosi; 55 René Stoeltie; 56 left V.T. Wonen/Spaarnestad/Utrecht/Holland; 56 right V.T. Wonen/Spaarnestad/Utrecht/Holland; 57 left Elizabeth Whiting & Associates; 57 right Simon McBride; 57 below Dominic Blackmore/Robert Harding Picture Library; 58-59 Paul Ryan (Architect: Ian Hay)/Conran Octopus; 59 right Guillaume de Laubier/S.I.P./Elizabeth Whiting & Associates; 60 Simon Brown/Interior World; 61 Elle Decoration/Simon Brown; 62 Mark Darley/Esto; 63 left Jean-Paul Bonhommet; 63 right Michael Freeman; 64 above Camera Press; 64 below Marianne Haas/Stylograph; 65 above left Simon Brown/Interior World; 65 above centre Elle Decoration/Simon Brown; 65 above right V.T. Wonen/Spaarnestad/Utrecht/Holland; 65 below left Elle Decoration/Simon Brown; 65 below right Elle Decoration/Simon Brown; 66 Elizabeth Whiting & Associates; 67 Mark Darley/Esto; 68-69 Dominique Vorillon; 69 right S. Couturier/Archipress; 70 Gionata Xerra (Designer: Marco Romanelli; Owner: Gabriella Gilli); 71 Mick Hales; 72-73 Camera Press; 73 right Roland Beauffre/Agence Top; 74 Elizabeth Whiting & Associates; 75 Marie Claire Maison/Nicolas Tosi; 76 Marie Claire Maison/Nicolas Tosi (Stylist: J. Borgeaud); 77 Paul Warchol.

AUTHOR'S ACKNOWLEDGMENTS

Without the terrific editorial team at Conran Octopus, the time I spent planning, researching and writing this book would have been less productive, and not nearly as enjoyable. I am especially grateful to: Jane Chapman, whose patient nature coexists with a ruthless eye for the inconsistent, the inelegant, the illogical and the misspelt; Alistair Plumb, who imposed elegance, order and clarity on these chapters and maintained his calm demeanour despite a schedule that would have driven lesser men to drink; and Claire Taylor, for fulfilling a particularly tricky picture-research brief with diligence and flair.

I would also like to thank John Wallace, Denny Hemming and my agent, Barbara Levy, without whose encouragement, counsel and support the solitary hours I spend in my own work space would be very much poorer.